D1525618

12 PRINCIPLES
TO INSTILL IN
YOUR YOUTH

By Leonard Washington III

Property of the
High Point Public Library

CONTENTS

This book is dedicated to all the mentors and family and friends I've had over the years who helped me be the person I was, the person I am and the person I will be, Thanks. To those that read this and it helps you please pass these concepts from generation to generation as applicable. Thank you

"If I have seen further, it is by standing on the shoulders of giants." – Sir Isaac Newton

CHAPTER 1:HONOR THY MOTHER AND THY FATHER

"HONOUR THY FATHER AND THY MOTHER: THAT
THY DAYS MAY BE LONG UPON THE LAND WHICH
THE LORD THY GOD GIVETH THEE."- (EXODUS
20:12..)

Some may think, "oh no, this is NOT the book for me, he is starting out preaching to me. Relax, everything that I believe may not work for you and vice versa. However, the things I am sharing with you here provide you the greatest strategies in your path to financial freedom, great friendships, less stressful situations and ultimately, peace within oneself – JOY

Pay respects to your mother and your father, why? Simply put, you would not be here if not for them. It took me years until I was responsible for myself to realize that no matter how good or bad things were, not only could my upbringing have been worse but that my parents made sacrifices so that I could be where I am today. The same shall be true for you as one day you may come to this conclusion but for now it is only natural to no put two and two together in your youth. Often times the ones that truly only care the most are your parents. Some of you may be thinking that this isn't the case for you. Perhaps your parents were not around or were horrible to you. To this I say, not only do I understand your misfortune but to consider those who did step into your life and serve the purpose of either figure.

My parents divorced at a young age and while my mother worked different jobs to provide for my sister and I, we still didn't have a strong enough support system. She did the best she could with what she had. I had a Godmother named Barbara. She made sure we had clothes for school, shoes and occasionally some mediocre video games for us to play (we had no internet in this time so it is not like she had a clue nor did I). I often felt like I wanted an older brother or someone to guide me into how to grow into a young man.

My father was around but not for the times where I needed him in development. This is not to slight him. The divorce on him was tough but it was also tough on my sister in I. Going to school or being amongst friends who had both parents and siblings and perhaps a pet. Not to mention various expense toys that I wasn't able to have but I digress. The key thing was family and education and that is what I will spend time emphasizing on in this book. The root of it all is family AND education. Yes, it is true, you can go far with one or the other but I will tell you that I could go much further with both.

I envied those around me who had what appeared to be a strong family unit not because I knew what that meant, but because they seemed on the surface to be happy. Sure they had some noticeable issues but what family didn't. Having both parents felt normal. The reality is, there really isn't a "normal" family. It takes a village to raise children and you rarely hear of the mentors, the step fathers, the uncles, the Godmothers, who stepped in and helped raise the youth. If you lack both parents or if you feel as though yours are not suitable you must seek out some of these individuals.

Focus your energy into things and people that bring out the best in you. You cannot choose your parents or your siblings but you CAN choose who you keep as your company, but we will touch on that subject a bit later. I had various mentors and teachers throughout life who showed me things I may have never learned even if I had the ideal family structure. Different cultures have different rules that they abide by too. Study what they do that may work and replace ones that you see that aren't beneficial for you.

Wisdom, while you are able to observe from your parental figures is FREE. You will eventually find your way paying for education in various courses in pursuit of a college degree or some sort of skill. Learning from them early sets you up better later. Malcolm Gladwell has a great book called "Outliers". In it he suggests 10,000 hours as a basis from the practice one needs to become great at any particular thing. It does not guarantee greatness but a head start never hurts. Those who have the family and education have this and you have to do what you can with what you have. Those who see potential in you do not mind helping you succeed. They take great honor in helping one become the best version of themselves. Therefore, you must honor those who made a way for you as you wished to be honored by those who will come after you as you move on. This is the circle of life.

CHAPTER 2:WHAT ANOTHER THINKS ISN'T YOUR BUSINESS!

"Mind your business!" - Everyone

This is a tough thing to adapt to because growing up no one walks around wishing everyone would hate them. That is a learned thing. Everyone wants to be loved, respected and admired. Learning to love yourself should be your goal. You may have been taught to listen to your elders and do as you are told. While that might be for your own well being, at a certain point those who you trusted to raise you should also instill in you the desire to think for yourself. Thinking for yourself means not constantly worrying about what others think of you. If you have done them no wrong and there is nothing you have done for them to be upset with you then why worry about it? Worry is mostly in ones head and often never even happens. Instead, put your energy into those that appreciate it.

To do this you have to accept that Perception IS reality. I would often hear this at the first job I had. I was never one to dwell on how I looked. My self-esteem was very poor growing up. Bad teeth, short in height, etc. I wore uniforms to school as a child so having to put more effort into my appearance wasn't something I was used to until high school. Going to college required more style to fit in but going to a job where I had to look professional was another ball game.

Looking the part is what allows others to feel comfortable around you - Solidarity. While wearing certain clothes is part of the game, the big part is how you come off when you behave around others. If you show up to work late every day, the thought might be that you are not punctual. If you make many mistakes in your emails it also reflects that you aren't very detailed.

People can assume you are this and that but you can prove them right or prove them wrong. Certain things you can't control but you can control your attitude. The truth is, that is the only real thing you are in control over. You can often get a desired outcome based off you keep composure. Will Smith, who was one of the nicest guys in Hollywood suddenly looked like a bully for attacking Chris Rock at the Oscars. Chris made a tasteless joke at Will's wife and Will reacted in a way that was negative. Some may say that they understood where Will was coming from but he was still in the wrong. Perception is still reality. We perceive him to be a bully therefore he is, even though for years he has not given you a reason to think that he was anything but a class act. This is the world we live in, I don't make the rules, I just report them.

While everyone makes these mistakes from time to time, you cannot make a habit of any of this in a professional setting and expect those to take you seriously. After all, this is a job. What you should do is practice being accountable early and often and in settings where you aren't being paid money. This ensures that these good habits rub off on you in a work environment and don't feel like a huge drain on you emotionally as you grow older. Often times schools focus on grades but really the grades aren't as important as discipline.

Discipline gives those watching you a good indication on whether or not they want to entertain your company or make you a friend. This could be a double edged sword as it could also attract those who will not match your efforts so be aware of this not just in professional relationships but romantic ones as well. Ask yourself, would you want to be with someone who doesn't make you feel like they are doing their best? If you answered no, then imagine this is how others may also feel when they think about you?

It took me many years to accept that saying for what it is because we often tell ourselves that someone else should not judge us as they do not know the whole story. The truth is, they don't care. You may be the bad guy in their story and vice versa. There isn't much you can do to change that outside of being a great person and even then that may not be enough. Being a great person for yourself is what you should strive towards. Not everyone is meant to like you but if you are a good person you should expect most to like you. Being liked and admired is a skill on its own. It is not something that naturally happens. Do NOT confuse being a good person with being liked and admired. You can be a good person and no one will care about what you do until you make a mistake. Likewise, you can be a bad person and if money and power is what those you seek approval from care about first and foremost then I would strongly encourage you to pick better friends.

CHAPTER 3:BUILD A BETTER BRIDGE (BEFORE YOU DESTROY ONE)

"Am I not destroying my enemies when I make friends with them?" – Abraham Lincoln

I believe he was quoted as saying something in line with in order to make friends one must be friendly, but I am not sure he [Lincoln] actually said that. The point is still true. A man believes he can go far alone but knows he could go farther with the help of others. Think back to Chapter 1. It is those that brought you up that helped you. It isn't as if you made yourself from the womb. No man is truly self made. I say that to say this, build as many bridges as you can and you will never be homeless. You never know who is watching so be kind, be friendly. I am not advising you to be manipulative and be friendly hoping that people will in turn do things for you. I do not believe the universe works that way. Often times you will find yourself doing things for people with no reward. It is bad that parents raise children with rewards for school work or chores as it eventually makes them entitled and expecting great things whenever they do something nice. It makes the man expect things from a woman for providing a meal, etc. Instead, you should do things simply because you enjoy doing them. That in itself is its own reward. I'm sure you may have heard some of these sayings before in other words and stories. I feel like the wisdom there is universal.

The homeless man whom asks for a few dollars is unlikely to pay you back or be able to do much for you. Who is to say that in the future that same person can run into you again and repay or do greater. Even more likely is that because you "Paid it forward", this person who was down on their luck may be able to help someone else who may be worse off than they were. Eventually the good that you put out into the world can come back when you need it. Don't look for it every time you do something but trust me. Have faith that when you need it the help you need will arrive in some way, shape or form.

Money can open some doors and close others but your network can do the same thing. People who have a big Networth often have a big Network. Don't be mislead in thinking that wealth just appeared out of nowhere. I am not saying that everyone with wealth worked hard for it or that opposite. What I am saying is that it came off the backs off someone at some point in time for those that have it. We will discuss later what you can do when it comes to finances but just know that having friends in high and low places can be strategic for you. Not everyone wealthy is going to help you just as you assume someone who is poor cannot help you.

People who have a skill and or a talent is invaluable. You can probably put a price on it but the price can be lower than of a friend than a stranger. What I mean to say is, that the man who is in charge of fixing the roof on your house is more likely to work out a better deal for you if he calls you a friend than the guy you called up from the hardware store that you just met today. Now that you understand the value of a friendship understand that enemies can become friends and vice versa. Take the high road with enemies so that they can become friends. That is the best approach when possible. Obviously there are those who you should just avoid at all costs especially if it could cost you your life. Those who you simply find as competition are often those who you can learn from and reach new heights. Iron sharpens iron, this is the result of joining forces, at least in theory.

For those that become enemies that were once friends you need to be careful. Truly look into why you are enemies in the first place. Is it something you can repair.

Do you value this friendship? Is it something minor or something major, was it a misunderstanding? Time can heal all wounds, but only if you both mature in time. In time try to extend the olive branch. Sometimes the person or persons are looking at you as solely being at fault and not seeing your perspective. If you reach out even if you don't see things that way you may be surprised as what the perceived issues were. They may not even have been issues at all. People go through things and hear things and it can influence them in ways that they normally wouldn't react to. Not everything has to do with you that someone is going through, always remember that. As you control your attitude and composure, your enemies will have to still maintain a level of respect for you and that goes a long way when it comes to repairing a friendship lost. Even if you repair the friendship it may never be the same but a bridge seldom traveled is better than a burned one you can't cross!

CHAPTER 4: MARCH BADNESS BRINGS APRIL TAXES

"April showers bring May flowers" – Thomas Tusser

I used to always wonder what that saying meant and where it came from. It wasn't until I was in my thirties that I bothered to even research it. What a time to be alive, to where you can just "google" search for information. Just a click of a button, no newspaper or Dewey decimal system. Just a thought and an answer, multiple answers to help you discern fact from fiction. The meaning of the line in question refers to the more rain the more flowers bloom as a result. This can go either way. Whatever you reap you sow. There are many sayings that are similar and the result is that you should be prepared and that the more prepared you are the better off you will be, even in the face of a bad outcome. When money increases, your blood pressure decreases, the same can be said when your money decreases.

Health is wealth, there is no substitute for that but we spend most of our lives in and out of boxes. From living in one to working in one just to eventually die in one. When you reduce life to those terms it should make you question what you are doing with your short time while you are here. Everyone on Earth present right now will all be gone in 200 years to simply be replaced by others and that cycle will repeat until I suppose there is no more Earth. Your attitude should be to enjoy your time here. I heard a great saying that says "Life is like an amusement park, enjoy all the rides you can, meet others enjoying things with you but when it is time for the park to close you have to go." Now I am not sure who to attribute that quote to as it may have been said by many and I am paraphrasing a bit to be honest but I was forever changed by reading that. Your life may not be an amusement park because you may look at those parks at being fun, or maybe you don't like them at all. In any case, every ride and attraction may not be your thing but there could be a few things you do enjoy.

Focus on those things because when it is over you want to at least know you left doing what you enjoyed. I say this saying that is all good as long as you haven't wronged anyone in doing what you wanted to do. That out of the way let us get back into the financial aspects of this chapter. True wealth means you have more opportunity to do the things you wish to do versus doing more things that you have to. When I worked for myself and worked from home during the Covid-19 pandemic some would say to me. "How can you always find time to do things you want?!" I would simply respond, "Some men do what they want, others do what they can." A bit harsh? Perhaps, but true nonetheless. I am not sure where I picked that up but tell me that the concept isn't refreshing. Having financial freedom and the ability to not worry about keeping your lights on or where your next meal is coming from allows you to focus on other things like travel and things you wish to upgrade and or replace. How do I get there? What should I be doing in my early years to even think about doing this? These are questions you may be asking or have considered. You need a plan.

One of the many popular job interview questions is "Where do you see yourself in five years?" It is hard to answer that because truthfully, no one knows, but we answer to appease the person asking. If you had a plan then you'd realize that a five year plan is really a one year plan with steps in between. That one year plan starts with a month plan. It doesn't just happen in five years let alone over night. Just as you have a plan for what you want to do with your time you should have a plan for what you'd like to do with your money. They say time IS money right? The time it takes to do your taxes is a stark reminder about death and taxes. You can only avoid them for so long until they catch up to you. The better you prepare yourself should allow you to handle them both easier. Sure one is more finite but you get the idea. Leaving control of your life in someone else's hands should concern you. This is why I said earlier that at a certain point you must think for yourself.

I loved my teachers in school but once school was over I felt as if I was lied to and had to unlearn many things.

I do not fault my teachers, they did what they could with what resources and information they had and did as they were instructed to do. Some wisdom is personal opinion and mine is that taxes should have been taught. Even if you are not great at doing them every person should be capable and be given the education on how to do them. That is more important than learning the circumference of a circle. In the old days you had to write all of this stuff down or retain it from memory because you were warned that there wouldn't be a device that displays all of this information. Joke is on those folks as I see 3.14 from the calculator on my iPhone. One could argue that technology makes us lazier and dumber but that is another conversation for another time. The actual skills you need to survive have been called electives and the things we don't even use daily have been the core courses for students.

We have been taught to work for someone else instead of for yourself. Thinking for yourself sets you free from this. Being poor is first in your head before it is ever in your wallet. Read that again if you need to. There are many great books out there that I've read over the years. If you are reading this book then I beg you to read more, read whatever you can but eventually read up on finances because you will be taken advantage of for years until you decide to take your life into your own hands this way. There is this thought that being rich makes you evil or a bad person. Understand that being rich and wealthy are different. Having more than enough for one person and more than enough for a small city are very very different. You work all year long to pay the government money that it did not help you earn only to receive a third of it. The less money you make the more they give you, as if you were rewarded for giving the government more of your money. Meanwhile the more money you make you could end up getting a third of it back. It sounds bizarre but that has happened to me.

Learn to understand tax brackets and how they work. I can't get into it much here as those can change frequently or not at all depending on who is running the country. What I can tell you is that the person at H&R block or Jackson Hewitt is not your enemy but they are not your friend either. A friend would fight for ALL tax breaks possible. Those guys expect you to hand in a W2 and be out of the chair in thirty minutes or less! I once was so proud of myself for saving up all of my receipts from EVERY purchase I made for the year of 2014. I walked into Jackson Hewitt and the woman who I waited 1 hour to help me scoffed at me saying I would have to pay her more to help me. I didn't understand at the time but I do now. She could have been more polite with rejection but there is a big difference between an itemized deduction and a standard deduction.

Learn the differences because while most people work a regular job and have one W2 they get basic breaks. If you work multiple jobs and travel a lot and rack up various expenses it might make more sense to itemize everything. Keeping receipts keeps you honest and more importantly keeps the IRS from auditing you if you have specific numbers in tact. I went home that day defeated and I felt like someone reduced my lively hood because I ended up not only owing money to the government but I had to pay the person who did my taxes money just to find out that I owed money. Had I had the knowledge myself I would have saved the 200 bucks and put that towards whatever money

I owed and even now I question if what was said that I owed was even accurate at all.

The sooner you learn how to handle your taxes the sooner you are able to redistribute that money into yourself. Into your businesses or family needs or whatever it is you need a lump some of money to do during the year. That new roof you need done? Your tax money is what you could have used. Many people buy new homes and cars with their money. Maybe you are behind on bills and credit cards. I am not telling you what to do with it (I would actually invest it depending on your situation) but just know that the more you have to use is the more you can use and its your money or your life!

CHAPTER 5: BUILD A BETTER BRIDGE (BEFORE YOU DESTROY ONE)

"With great power comes great responsibility" – Stan Lee

One of the biggest things I wished I knew about early on in life was the importance of credit. As a child you are always taught that you have got to save your money for the things you want but what if I told you that you could borrow money until you have enough to get the things you couldn't afford at the time? You'd say, "Sign me up!" or, "Sounds too good to be true" You could be glass half empty of half full but you should take heed to both thoughts. Credit, like money isn't bad, you just have to be taught how to use it to work for you. You can chase money to build credit or build credit to chase money and that loop can continue beyond your death (some types of credit pass over to your loved ones). The power of credit is the opportunity to open doors that would normally be closed. What if your car breaks down on you one day? You can try to fix the car yourself and or pay someone. Depending on how serious the issue is you may just replace the car. In either case it may cost you a bunch of money that you don't have or can't afford to part with right now. The remedy here is to have good credit.

I grew up hearing the term "Good Credit" but what exactly is it. Folks mentioned good credit, as if it was something to be desired. It was like a part of what made you attractive, like an award winning smile or personality. Having good credit is often associated with those who are rich. Don't be mistaken. Good credit doesn't mean one is rich, it simply means they made great choices with their credit or just haven't got around to making mistakes with it yet. Many tend to mess up their credit as they are in college and spend their post graduate years trying to fix it. Maybe you had children or just lost your job. A divorce could also be a financial disaster. Falling behind on bills isn't fun. One week you have money to pay something back and then you forget about it or the age old saying. "Rob Peter to pay Paul". This is how it starts, all with good intentions but bad timing.

The question then is, do you start out with good credit and then it gets worse? Not necessarily. You may have no credit at all and need something to start it out. What I implore you to do is if you have children, add them on a line of your credit as an Authorized User. They do not need a credit card yet, I repeat, do not give them a card. What you are doing here is setting them up to hit the ground running. The better credit you start with the better types of credit cards and loans become available to you without even having to prove anything to creditors. It will all be on the strength of YOUR credit. You can do this for friends you trust or anyone close. This is called "Credit Piggybacking" If I knew of this sooner I would have asked for it to happen much earlier. It wasn't until I found this information online around the time of purchasing my first house.

My stepfather Gideon had excellent credit and I had to explain to him what I was trying to do. He was unsure at first as even he had never heard of such a concept. I assured him that I would not need a credit card. I would simply be utilizing his long credit history and as it shows up on my credit report it reflects on me as if I had also held down a credit card responsibly. Doing this allowed me to get better credit cards and finally achieve my goal of getting a home. I am forever grateful to you Gideon. These are secrets that most don't talk about but here I am sharing it with you. Use this knowledge and prepare the future generation. Seek out those who have good credit and perhaps they will accept payment to piggyback off of their credit or if they are nice do it for free. Good credit gives you good interest rates. Interest can sometimes cost you almost as much as the item you are trying to own. A house with a 5 percent interest rate will cost you thousands of more dollars over time than one with a 3 percent interest rate. Student loans are often a problem for many students and yet those loans have the lowest amount of interest. Use those loans wisely because you may end up paying for them for the rest of your life. The problem with the loans is that you were told you would find work proportionate to the amount your education cost you. You thought you were going to become an engineer and instead you worked at a bakery for a year. Trust me, you have to have a plan for your money and credit should be what you use as shield.

They say cash is king! Why risk getting into crazy credit card debt when you can simply use what you have and if you don't have it you don't need it. That way of thinking may be fine if you are wanting a new pair of shoes but it doesn't get a bank to trust you with a home loan. Need a new roof on your house. Good luck saving $5000 for it. Even if you had that kind of money saved, why use it all at once when you don't have to.

This is what I call the Great Credit Opportunity. You see, your money IS king. The pawns go first in chess. Likewise, you should be using your credit first. The better you advance your credit the more cash you end up acquiring with higher credit limits. This means you can borrow money without first using your own to get what you want. Had any of this been explained to me early it would have saved me years of hurdles and financial suffering. I may not have understood it at year age either but it wasn't even explained at all! Oh how I wish I could go back and change that but things are what they are and it is never too late to learn. Your credit score can vary from bureau to bureau. This is because they report at different times and don't always have the same things being reported to them. The trick here is to look into which lenders use which bureau and try to make sure you are in good standing. You can use various apps and or websites that provide an idea of what you score is and what you can do to improve them for FREE.

As I repaired my credit I would look at those sites almost daily as my obsession for improvement was exhilarating but sometimes exhausting. In the end you must balance being diligent and yet patient. These scores can get drastically worse overnight but can take years to gain back what you lost over several missed payments or charge offs. When speaking of those two things they are obviously negative. Any negative items show you have a lack of responsibility to lenders.

Never pay these items back in full. I know you are told you should but if they are already hurting you, paying them in full doesn't help you at all. Try to negotiate with the lender. If they have already sold your account into Collections then I would wager that they would rather have something from you than nothing at all. I myself didn't believe such an option existed until I tried it myself and they will play ball if you play hard ball. Do not jump at the first offer. Depending on when you ask and how polite you are you may get anywhere from 30 percent off to 60 percent off of what you owe. Your mileage may vary.

So why didn't this come up when I was a child? May be for the same reasons that you may not have been aware. Finances are very taboo. No one wants to compare their money or the lack thereof to others. After all, rich people are often portrayed as selfish and evil on television and movies and I'm not saying that they all aren't or that they all are. All I am pointing out is that it is easier to get money when you already have it. Credit works the same way, those with good credit don't really need it. It is those of us with subpar credit or bad credit that often need it the most. Seek out cards that offer travel rewards and cash back. These are the cards often exclusive to those with good scores as they can be more selective with whom they do business with. I often wondered how the credit card companies stay in business.

Many fall behind and are charged interest but businesses who accept credit cards are charged a fee too. You, the consumer get nothing in return but you could travel the world free if only you had good credit and a great credit card. Notice that when you use cash you also get nothing but at least a credit card with no rewards helps you to establish credit. Use your debit card at a gas station and get your account hacked, well the bank holds you some what responsible and may only return some of your money.

Credit cards on the other hand reimburse EVERYTHING. You should use credit to protect your money so that you can save most of it. One key thing that a lot of these financial gurus may not suggest is to match your monthly bills with that of credit cards. You SHOULD pay your bills anyway, why not get cash back rewards and the like for them? You get nothing for your cash in return. Doing this allows you to focus on paying YOURSELF first. This is how you can save without trying to having a lower way of living. Do NOT increase your expenses doing this, keep them exactly the same. Now that you are using these tactics that then brings up the next question. What are you saving it for exactly?

CHAPTER 6:SAVING MONEY IS NOT ENOUGH

"You can't take it with you..." - Various

Sure that is a quote from someone at some point in history but no matter how many times it has been said it is still a reality. So you've got your credit together and you have saved a bunch of money, now what? You don't need a yacht or a bigger house. The more money you make the more problems you see? Why though? It is likely because the human want does not end simply because you have more. Some say less is more. Less risk means less opportunity to fail but you have to remember that there isn't risk without reward. You have to invest your money is what I am trying to tell you.

A savings account with your local bank or credit union is great for an emergency. Did you lose your job? Maybe you need to pay bills for six months and maxing out your credit cards just isn't an option. In the last chapter we discussed using credit as a shield for your money but this is only when you HAVE money to pay it back. When you do not this is a concern as you have money sitting in an account that isn't serving you. It is simply there in case you need it. You have to use the EXTRA money to do as your credit does for you when you earn rewards—make money for you. You can invest in the stock market which is risky, you can learn to do it at a smaller scale and see what happens.

For years I had small stock and forgot about it as time went on and I changed jobs. I never once thought about what the market was doing. I was only concerned about paying bills as I was living check to check. You were not put here to simply pay bills and die. What does it matter to be rich if you do not have the freedom to move as you want to. Money comes and goes and it goes even faster if you spend more than you earn. Millions of dollars can go through your hands in years without you even retaining a half of it. I would often sit back, satisfied that I survived the month and all of my bills were paid. I would try to hold onto whatever money was left over (after treating myself to nice food and entertainment of course) and plot on how I could perhaps save next paycheck and thus make saving easier for me. Sometimes this would happen but then life would play its hand and then I would be back to square one. Sound familiar?

Do you find yourself in this situation? Did you escape this hamster wheel type of living and the thought of it takes you back to a different part of your life? Just as you lend money to a friend, you must only lend with the idea that you may never see it again. Investing your money has to have the similar type of thought except you hope to get this money back. It isn't really gone but it really isn't in your control if you wish to not be taxed heavily from taking it out too fast. Inflation goes up but your living expenses may never match it. It is set up that way as the dollar is worth less with inflation and the more money circling means the less it is worth to those who have the power. You are at a disadvantage and we will learn more about that shortly. Back to saving you have to understand that you have to think outside the box if you wish to win.

You cannot be afraid to lose money if you wish to make money. Understand that 0.01% interest on $1000 will take years to amount to anything, you may not even live to see it do anything for you. What if you took that same $1000 and placed it into stock that offer 3 percent yield or 5 percent yield. Imagine taking that $1000 and adding another $2000. Suddenly your money is growing without you doing anything different aside from adding more money to it. The compounded interest over time means you can retire from working sooner. This means more time for your family and hobbies and not at the expense of your remaining years in life.

Most retire and have to life off of what they saved. You should try to retire with money still coming in in different forms of supplemental income. This could be renting out a home or taking on a small level skill that pays your smaller bills as your home loans and car loans and children have all been taken care of. It is not about how much you earn either, it is about how much you are able to save but know that that means nothing without investing.

Saving money is NOT enough when you lack a plan for it. In order to really develop a plan don't just do what everyone else tells you, even me in this book. Invest in yourself by educating yourself on what you want to do with your life. You need to be aware of your strengths and how to play to them so that you can perhaps earn income from them. Do this even if it means you will have to do it for free for a while. When you are truly good at something it won't feel like hard work. That isn't to say it won't be hard work but that you wouldn't feel like you are giving as much of your time, energy and effort into it (even though you are without realizing) as you would on a job you care much less about. You should take a good look at yourself in the mirror and be honest.

CHAPTER 7: SELF AWARENESS IS KEY

"To thine own self be true" – William Shakespeare

Y ou must be yourself. I know, I know, that is as cliché as it gets but it is still true. Some people think they are being themselves but what they actually doing is being what they believe others want them to be. This could be a parent or a lover or a boss. Some could argue it could be a religious figure. Whatever the case may be, if you fail to be you, you aren't really living at all. I am not saying do not listen to those with influence and principles.

What I am saying is that you can do those things and still follow them and have your own personality and way of life. You can only pretend to be something you aren't not for so long until you become overwhelmed with depression the very minute you lack direction and a support system to pick you back up when you are down. Ever been dumped by a boyfriend or girlfriend before?

Failed an exam or got fired from a job? Comfort food helps, but what helps the best is knowing yourself and being aware of who you are. How else can you become a better version of you for a better person who deserves you? We will touch more on relationships in another chapter but I want to change gears slightly. I have been talking in generalities for a bit but I will to be very direct. Now I may lose some of you as in a minute or so I am going to start talking specifically to those who grew up poor. I am going to talk specifically to those who have been disenfranchised. I am doing to start talking specifically to those that look like me.

You are at a disadvantage..

Let's look back at credit. Some of us had parents who may have had the opportunity and knowledge to put you on their credit early. Some of our parents may have had bad credit and could not do so. Then they are some who just didn't know. Knowledge is power!

Take a look at this right here:

Average FICO Score by Race		
Race	2019 Average Score	Classification
Black	677	Good

Hispanic	701	Good
Other	732	Good
White	734	Good
Asian	745	Very Good

Source: Shift Credit Card Processing, August 2021, reporting U.S. Federal Reserve data

Now what does this tell us? It shows that Black Americans have a much lower credit score than other ethnicities on average. The pay way to the American dream is being a home owner. If having good or great credit is the pathway to homeownership then we have work to do. You must take this information and improve your credit. Generations ago everyone knows we had slavery of African Americans in the United States of America. That goes without saying. I am not going to discuss reparations or anything of that nature here. I will tell you that ever since then the financial system favors those who have money and power over those who do not. Ever play Mario Kart? The person in first place gets the banana or worse items. The folks who are behind get greater items to even the odds. Now I don't think giving folks who are on top a raw deal is the answer to the problem but the folks at a disadvantage have come from those who had a raw deal and money is needed to fix the situation. Not just money though, family and an education is what is needed to break the generational curses of poverty.

Many will blame this person and that person but at the end of the day you have to be responsible for you. You were randomly chosen to be what you are, remember that. So be okay with being you first over being a group or this or that. By and large we are mostly the same in our wants and needs as human beings, but you are to experience things in your own unique way. You can't that if you limit your way of life, thinking and opportunities to what the world says you are or where you come from. Knowing this you should attempt to acquire solid friendships and land. Not simply items to look rich but items that are assests that allow your children and their children's children to be rich.

Imagine if you will that you are playing the board game Monopoly. Familiarize yourself with that game if you have not already as it pretty much explains the way the current way capitalism works in the united states to a degree. A few players travel the board acquiring wealth and various properties which generate more wealth once others land on said property. What does that mean here in what we are discussing? Picture yourself in Jim Crow America where you are now free but still looked down upon. All men were created equal yet you were not even thought of in that statement. The idea that you were going to have your own businesses and property and people to land on your "square" was not even thought of. Why should those who look like you go to your place of business if it costs more than going to those who have been in business longer than you?

This is how the money in black communities continues to disappear faster than in other communities. Sure, you could start supporting more black businesses. It doesn't matter what your background is to help. Don't simply help because they are black, help because you understand the root of the problem with poverty in this country. So for those of you looking for change. Start with being self-aware with where you may have started financially. If you are someone that looks like me, you have to work a little bit harder to get where some of our brothers and sisters are and although unfair it is okay. Do not point fingers and blame. Work with those willing to help. If you benefited from the past. Be willing to be more understanding and helpful and not ignorant and guilty over things you had no direct part in. Accepting that you benefited indirectly from the past allows us to come together and move forward.

Aside from things like money and race, perhaps your appearance is something you are focused on. You can't really control that either, well, I guess you could with money but you will have to learn to have a tough skin on those things you are insecure about until then. I was very insecure about my height, my teeth and my flat feet. Eventually I realized that I have to be happy with myself first. If I let my self- esteem become so poor that it reflected on how I interacted with others could you really fault someone for not wanting to be around? Learn to embrace your shortcomings. You do not have to accept them as limitations if you do not allow them to limit you into what you want to do. I am constantly talking to people on video and in person for a living. Had I kept my fear of what others thought about me from allowing me to speak then I wouldn't be here now able to guide you to your fulfilling your dreams.

CHAPTER 8:HAPPINESS IS YOUR RESPONSIBILITY

"True happiness is a self manifestation"
– Leonard Washington III

Normally I would have a quote here but happiness can be different things for different people and I think you should figure out what that is for you. Lots of people can tell you what happiness and how to describe it. You know what sadness is, and you know what joy is, but to me to truly be happy is to not worry about being happy. It is simply being in a state of joy with the choices you make. It is better to be in degrees of happiness than to go around searching for it. Happiness is said to already be within. You want to know why that is true? It is because nothing can truly make you happy long term. Do you remember that toy you got at five years old that you told your parents would make you happy? I would wager that you don' t even think about the gift, let alone remember what it was. This is because the idea of something is more appealing than the thing itself. People are the same way. What makes you think that if an object without feelings or a personality could stop making you happy that a person with those qualities eventually would too? That isn't to say that people can't make you happy in moments, but ultimately if you are not happy with yourself then nothing they do for you ultimately matters. They can add in your happiness and help remove things from your life that make you unhappy but it is always unwise to try to put your hopes into someone for your happiness.

The marriage/divorce rate in the United States is almost fifty percent. Many will say that times were different and we didn't have all the distractions of technology to aid in divorce. That may be true to an extent as it is easier to move on when you can swipe left or right and meet people easier through the internet. People didn't stay together because there was a lack of technology, they did so because there was more shame in divorce because of religious affiliation and stigmas surrounding being a single parent. This was a scarlet letter to women who may have already been a stay at home mother and or home maker. Women today, while still not having equal pay, make more than years prior and are comfortable taking on the roles of a single parent. Does this mean that women were happier generations ago? I cannot say, but I do feel as though the way technology can be used can make one unhappy. If you find yourself constantly comparing yourself to others and always looking for more than this can give room for attention towards other people and things instead of your partner and or family.

I remember growing up believing that I would be happy like others appear to be happy if I had what they had. Once I got what they had I wasn't as happy as I thought. Was the grass greener on the other side? Perhaps, but what is meant for others isn't always meant for you or right for you. Everything in due time. What happens here is that you are enchanted with the IDEA of being happy, not happiness itself. There is nothing wrong with wanting more, but people who are happy are often content with what they've got and if they don't get whatever thing it is they "want" they are fine just moving along. They aren't waiting around for Santa or someone else to drop off something to them. They aren't waiting around for some special person to come into their life. They just keep moving and doing things that they are in control of that they enjoy. The rest of it comes along with that as what you enjoy is often what you will attract!

Happiness is YOUR responsibility. It is not a place or a destination it is a state of balance. It is knowing that no matter what happens, you have seen enough of life to understand that problems are opportunities to improve. When you start looking at things that way you will be less affected by things that you can't control. Death unfortunately is a part of life. The other side of that is that you should make the most of the time you have here so that when it is over you won't feel as though you haven't done enough.

CHAPTER 9 : YOU MUST TRY

"You miss one hundred percent of the shots you don't take."-
Wayne Gretzky

Maybe you've heard that quote before somewhere. Perhaps from some bumbling office manager or your high school sports coach years ago. It is a powerful quote because nothing happens if you don't try. That girl or guy that you are interested in but scared to talk to. That Song you think you could sing better than someone else at karaoke. How about that job promotion you've wanted for years but wouldn't even apply for? Those things never come true for you without you making an effort and trying. Now I am not saying these things are going to be easy or that they will work out simply because you tried. However, the confidence boost from trying pays for itself. You must get used to rejection.

Not everyone nor everything is going to be for you. The sooner you accept this the sooner you can get going on the things meant for you. With a good attitude, some effort and the right people around you can go miles beyond the feet that you may get without those things. Don't be that person I see all the time that blames other people for their problems. You know that person who constantly makes excuses by saying their mom is at fault or this group is holding me back or I would have got something done had someone or some other thing helped me out. While I hear all of those comments, in time you will realize that no people care. If you really want something bad enough you have to go after it. A wise person once told me, "If you wait on your friends to do something you may never do what it is you want to do".

I never really thought about it because I was usually the friend who had money but no time to do things or had no money but plenty of time to do things in my twenties. There were lots of little things I wanted to do like going to a movie. I would never go to a movie alone but nowadays I enjoy the solitude. You came into this world alone (unless you are a twin or triplet, etc.) and you will likely leave alone. You will get many chances to try things over and over again but not if you don't initially try. Failure is painful but not as painful as not trying. One of the biggest questions I ask older people is what would they do over. Few say they would do much over but they many share that they regret not doing certain dreams they wanted out of fear of failure or that they regret not spending enough time with family. Do not be guided by fear. This is easier said than done but those who do not get persuaded by it usually end up on the winning side of things. Did the stock market crash and you sell everything? Guess who is going to make money? The people who saw the opportunity to TRY and make more money off of the bad situation. Many times people are afraid to try because they focus more on the bad and not on the good. Conversely, they don't think about learning from the experience if they fail.

This is important to understand because I feel as a young Black youth, I wasn't given many chances to fail. I was representing not just myself, but ALL Black people with my opportunities. Do not allow yourself to succumb to this way of thinking but keep it in mind as you sometimes become the gatekeeper for others who may not get a chance just because they look like you and you did not do a great job with whatever experience you were given. I am not saying it is fair at all, just to be aware and take note. The takeaway here is that even in failure you can look back and say' "Well at least I tried" and have a sense of assurance that you had the experience, it is over and for better or worse perhaps you want to do it again or never want to, but at least you know now. Spending the rest of your life wondering what could have been is not healthy. If you do not try, you ultimately have only yourself to blame.

CHAPTER 10:LET IT GO...

"Let It Be" – Paul McCartney

I f I just got the song from the animated film, Frozen, stuck in your head. You are very welcome. To the rest of you, do not attempt to google what I am talking about and suffer the same consequences. As a kid I was always told by my teachers to let things go. It is very hard to just 'let it go". What does that even mean? It often meant conceding, losing. Losing an argument or letting someone else play a video game even though it was actually my turn. The same folks that told me to never give up would at the same time tell me to let things go. It wasn't until I was much older where I saw what the benefit of this actually was. Letting things go is the BEST thing you can do for yourself. Your mental health is very important and often taken for granted. We have been taught to give everything our all and to do our best to win. While that is a great perspective, have you ever stopped and asked yourself at what cost?

What does it mean to try to win at everything and be mentally drained or stressed to the point of hospitalization? Winning a sport or some competition is one thing, but this behavior can spread into other areas of your life such as your job (unless your job is one of those things) and your relationships with friends and your spouse. There is a saying that I recall hearing, "learn to lose". To do this you must accept that the answer isn't always winning but allowing someone else to feel validated by winning so that both parties can move on. Perhaps you and your husband or wife had a bad argument and although you felt you were in the right you knew it wasn't worth arguing over and to let them have their way.

Sometimes this is what you may do to keep the peace. This can be advantageous in the work place too. In those environments you will have many people all with their own egos wanting to be heard and to be right with their opinions.

Learning to lose doesn't mean you become a doormat and let folks walk all over you. It is simply being strategic about what you feel is worth arguing over; you must pick your battles. Not every battle is worth arguing days on end just to prove a point. It is easier to just agree to disagree and focus on common ground. Not everyone was raised the same way or have the same life experiences so you must keep that in mind. I have had relationships in years past that might have went further had I sat back and took a moment to think about what the point of the argument was.

Often times I wanted to be certain that I was heard but I also wasn't listening as much. It is important to do that and as we discussed earlier to not take things personal. What happens is, when you get a bit testy you end up saying things you do not mean and or should not have said. Sometimes you will just not get across to others because they are you and their perception if you is skewed in a way that they wont allow themselves to concede to your point of view.

Ultimately, you'll see that learning to lose isn't really losing at all. It is realizing that what is true for YOU is not going to be true for others. It really doesn't have to be either as you free yourself by just letting someone else think what they want to think. People may disagree with you today and or disagree with you tomorrow. You might realize that your view in an argument was wrong. Therefore, do not let a disagreement turn into something big if it really isn't that big of a deal. At the end of the day people change their minds all the time.

CHAPTER 11:TO CHANGE

"Everyone complains about the weather but no one does anything about it" – Mark Twain

The more things change, the less they stay the same. Do you agree with that? Why or why not?

Now this last statement is a bit obvious to many because the reality is that things always change. We don't like change but change can be very subtle and it can be very quick without warning. You have to be prepared for it as you yourself will change a lot in your life time. We all lie to ourselves saying that we are always the same and don't "switch up" but to change is to evolve. To evolve is to grow. To change is part of life. Old ways and habits, while consistent may not always apply today, tomorrow or the day after. Get used to trying new things and trying to adapt to new situations. People don't like change because it roots them out of what they are comfortable with, even if they do NOT like what it is that is going on. At a certain point they just accept things for what they are. It is those that do not do this and try to find another way that often become successful. You have to be comfortable being uncomfortable.

Seek out changes within your own life and then you can be more comfortable with the changes around you that you cannot control. Your job might change, your relationship might end, you could move to a new area. One of the toughest things to endure is the loss of a loved one or a friend that you are no longer friends with. These are changes that you focus much more of your energy and time on instead of the ones that you should focus on. It is easier said than done but you must remember this. The one constant is as always, your attitude. If you can change a negative into a positive you will be better for doing so EVERY time.

We all at some point are often are asked, "What would be the one thing you would change about yourself?" People have various answers, those who say nothing are kidding themselves. We all have things we would change about ourselves so why settle for things we are just "Okay" with. I challenge you to find one thing about yourself that isn't necessarily bad, but that you could improve upon and work towards that. The progress that you make will not only be worth it, but it can push you to do more. You only appreciate what you have changed by appreciating first the opportunity to change it. The point here that I am trying to make is that change isn't always bad. You have to reframe your mind to look at change as an opportunity to do something different, something better.

CHAPTER 12:
TO FORGIVE...

"Forgiveness is the final form of love." – Reinhold Niebuhr

I remember as a child being taught how to pray. I understood an eye for an eye without being taught. You knocked down my legos, I will knock down yours. You ate my slice of pizza. I will eat yours next time and so on. That just seemed fair right? Perhaps, but it did not feel good outside of a message being received to whomever wronged you. As we get older and wiser we realize that an eye for an eye just means both people need eye patches now. How then does forgiveness become the final form of love?

Love in itself is hard. Many people spend their whole lives seeking love and or wanting to be loved and never even love themselves. Some of the reasons are the lack of the things mentioned in Chapters 1 through 9. Yes we have spent a great portion of time discussing finances and your attitude and so forth. All of these things are part of loving yourself. If you really loved yourself you would want to be in a position to do what you feel is right by yourself. No one else is going to do that for you. A lot of times you will find yourself doing things for others that cannot and or will not do the same for you. People will let you down and betray you. Not taking these transgressions personally are what help you to forgive. You forgive others so that you can be forgiven. This is what some of the prayers say to do. After all, no one is perfect and we are all bad in someone else's story so you must keep an open mind. Some would say who cares? And that the ends justify the means. Those who argue those points likely don't sleep well at night and if they do, it is not without security cameras and guards watching over them.

The truth is, to really forgive is to let go. Those who have wronged you live in your head and pay not rent. You may even think about them entirely too much so where it causes you enormous stress. Meanwhile the offending party isn't even thinking about you. It may eat them up inside and perhaps neither of you are able to confront each other and hash out things but part of that is arriving at different points of understanding in time. What I mean to say is, is that we are all vibrating on various frequencies. Some will find others on the same wavelength, and also find others who are not. It doesn't make those who are on different wavelengths bad people, they just may be in different places in life just as you once were. Take that into consideration as to forgive is easier when you understand.

What happens when you don't understand? It is easy to say if this is a simple quarrel and not something serious like financial ruin or something that results in death. It is as this point where you must come to the conclusion that forgiveness is not for THEM. It is for YOU. I know it sounds backwards but the situation has happened. It in most cases cannot be undone. All you can do is move on and move forward. The best way is to learn (from the situation), forgive, but do not forget. Keeping your distance is best for not only your safety but for your sanity as well. Forgiveness is for you so that you can heal. If you go through life not being able to forgive then the power of networking and friendship is something you may not have fortune in. Few make friends and have no issues. Perhaps you paid attention earlier and chose your friends wisely. If so, consider yourself lucky.

Forgiving is hard especially when there is trust involved. There are times when someone does you wrong and it hurts. However, when it comes to those you are in the company you keep, you can become bitter to the whole world around you. Why be bitter when you can become better? Those watching you may think twice about you as a person. At the time you may not care about those perceptions but again, forgiveness is for you. You have to forgive yourself first. If you forgive yourself first, you can accept that not all people will do you wrong doing as this person or group has.

I hope these lessons you take with you and pass on to generations to come. It is important to have any advantages you can in this thing we call life. You get the most out of it when you have the most knowledge of how things work for and against you early on. I enjoyed creating this and I hope you enjoyed reading. Now if you don't mind, I hope you can forgive me for having nothing left to add. God bless you

Prologue
In Summary

Chapter 1: Honor Thy Mother and Thy Father

The idea here is to respect those who came before you. They have the knowledge and wisdom of what worked to make things easier and smoother for you. They may not know everything and have all of the right answers but they know more than you. They can at least steer you in the right direction and give you perspective. They say there aren't any shortcuts in life. I would say that having a good guide to make some sense of this thing we call life is a close way to a shortcut. Sure, there are older folks who don't want to see you do better than them but I'd say the majority want to see the youth succeed. Nothing upsets them more than to see the youth squander the sacrifices they made in exchange for their time and money than for the world to not be better for those around them.

Chapter 2: What Another thinks isn't your business!

Just as the title says, don't worry about what another thinks of you. Most of these people don't pay your bills or help you anyway. That isn't to say that those are the only people you should worry about when it comes to opinions but that you should not sit around wondering how everyone feels about you. You are different things to different people at different times. Focus on what you think of yourself and how to make that better.

Chapter 3: Build A Better Bridge (Before Destroying One)

The point I was trying to make here is to try to salvage a relationship before getting into your emotions and destroying it. You are only in control of yourself, and as long as you can do that you have a fifty percent chance of showing someone to work with you than against you. Create friendships with strong foundations and it will take much to end them. Build friendships with surface level wants and needs and they are sure to crumble.

Chapter 4: March Badness Brings April Taxes

The lesson here is to be prepared. Things happen in seasons and not overnight. You should make the most out of certain weeks and months based on what is expected. The better you become at this the less hard you have to work on a return on investment.

Chapter 5: The Great Credit Opportunity

Credit ratings were created not long ago. Two systems exist as of this writing. FICO is based in California and the company was founded in 1956 by an engineer, Bill Fair, and a mathematician, Earl Isaac. VantageScore Solutions, based in Connecticut, was jointly founded by the current three bureaus, Equifax, TransUnion and Experian in 2006. These analytically computed numbers can control how much money you have access to in your life time. The earlier you understand and start getting these scores at their highest, the more opportunity you have to stop chasing money and allow money to grow by saving and investing.

Chapter 6: Saving Money is NOT Enough

We have been taught wrong models of how life should work financially. Did you believe that just adding money to your savings account every month was how you get rich? You aren't alone, millions of people are in that same boat while those who access to great credit cards and loans are able to hold onto their money and invest it while you simply grow pennies from a savings account each month. You must make your money make money for you, even while you sleep!

Chapter 7: Self Awareness is Key

Know who you are. Know what you are good and not great at and accept that. Accepting it doesn't mean not working at it. Be realistic with yourself and it won't bother you one someone else reaffirms these things. It should also not bother you if you get feedback that is NOT accurate. In this life you can prove people right or prove them wrong. The choice is yours.

Chapter 8: Happiness is Your Responsibility

Not a lot needs to be said here. If you want to be happy it is up to you and not some other person or thing. You have to get out of your own way to decide to be happy first. Second you must do all you can to protect your joy.

Chapter 9: You Must Try

The concept here is to actually do something about what you want done. Do not wait around for things to just happen. Before you point your fingers at others be sure you are doing your part to the best of YOUR ability.

Chapter 10: Let It Go

You have got to learn to let certain things go as it is unhealthy to hold on to things that don't serve you and your purpose. Not every battle is worth fighting to be tactful with what you choose to stand on.

Chapter 11: To Change

Things change, people change, but remember that you are a person that changes all the time too. Many reject changes, no one likes it at first but you must be willing to change to keep up with what is current if you wish to stay moving forward. Focus on changing things for YOU not for someone else.

Chapter 12: To Forgive

Forgive others so that you yourself may be forgiven is a popular biblical saying. I am saying that you should forgive others so that you can forgive yourself in situations that you feel guilt or had part in.

THE END

ACKNOWLEDGEMENTS

The ideas in this book were inspired by a concept I read online which stated that if the elders in a family were to transcribe family wisdom your history would never be lost. This is my attempt at sharing my legacy with those after my last days in hopes that this could help not only them now, but all who want a hopeful tomorrow.

ABOUT THE AUTHOR

Leonard Washington III was born in Hamden, CT in 1983. Leonard went to St. Thomas Day School in New Haven, CT and it was there that he was able to see families both rich and poor, black and white, etc. After moving to North Carolina in 1996 he would learn more about diversity in people and how education and family background plays an important part in the development of the youth.

Made in the USA
Columbia, SC
22 June 2022

62079871R00040